Roman Life

Contents

Written by Liz Miles

Illustrated by Rudolf Farkas

Collins

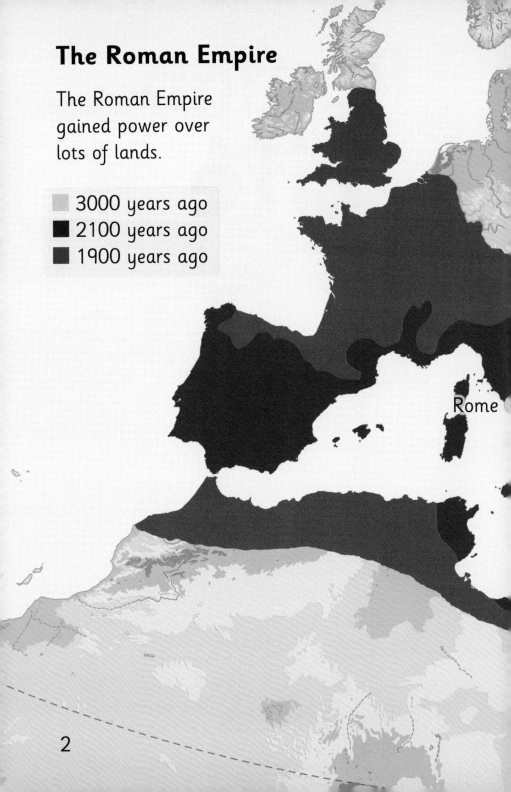

The Roman Empire

The Roman Empire
gained power over
lots of lands.

3000 years ago
2100 years ago
1900 years ago

Rome

3

Rome

Rome is about 3000 years old. It grew alongside the river Tiber. Thousands of people lived there.

forum for debates

Find out what life was like for people in Rome over 1900 years ago.

arenas for combat games and sports

river Tiber

Romans at home

Some Romans lived in **villas** with big rooms and enclosed gardens.

remains of a villa

Most Romans lived in crowded flats.

Rome had **sewers** and public toilets. Rich Romans had underground heating at home. They even had a room for bathing.

underground heating

sewer

Most Romans bathed at public pools.

public toilets

9

Roman people

Roman families could be big! Old people and children might all stay together. Most females stayed at home to cook and clean.

Females did spinning to make cloth.

Rich Romans had servants to clean their homes and cook. Some servants were enslaved people.

a **fresco** of an enslaved girl

Males had the most power and females could not vote.

But some females rose up, too. This empress spoke up for people's **rights**.

Some enslaved people could save up to get their freedom, but this did not happen often. Most spent their whole lives enslaved.

an enslaved man being freed

Some freed people went on to take jobs like baking or farming.

Entertainment

The Colosseum held 50,000 people. Crowds piled in to see violent "games".

Colosseum remains

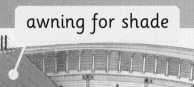

awning for shade

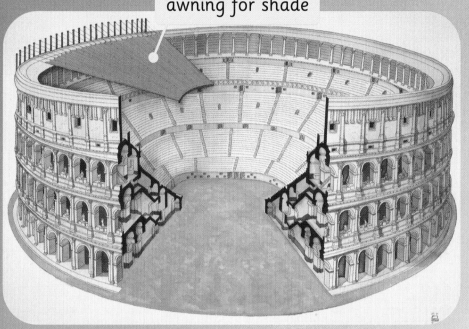

Some fighters used nets
and tridents.

These females chose
a fighter's life to
be independent.

Roman art tells us that lions and tigers might fight in the arena.

Wild beasts were kept in underground chambers and were lifted up to enter the arena.

These ropes drew the beasts up.

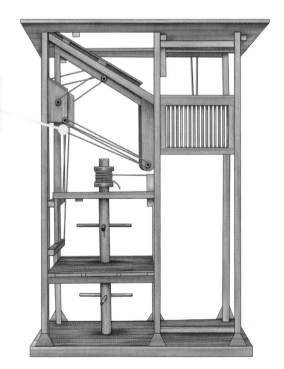

Some wild beasts took part in fights, but some were trained to do tricks to amuse the crowd.

They used crocodiles and antelopes for hunting games, too.

Thousands of wild beasts perished in the games.

Things the Romans left behind

coins

mosaics

pipes

toilets

statues

roads

debates meetings held to discuss things

forum an outside zone for meetings

fresco a kind of painting

rights things that people should be allowed to have or to do

sewers underground channels that take waste matter and rain water away

villas big Roman houses

Roman life

Review: After reading

Use your assessment from hearing the children read to choose any GPCs, words or tricky words that need additional practice.

Read 1: Decoding

- Turn to pages 6 and 7 and challenge the children to find the words that contain the /oa/ sound. Can they identify the spelling of the /oa/ sound? (*R__o__mans, encl__o__s__e__d, m__o__st*)
  - ○ Repeat for the /igh/ sound on pages 18 and 19. (*f__igh__ters, pr__i__ze, f__igh__t, tr__i__dents*)
- Point to captions for the children to read aloud. To encourage fluent reading, say: Can you blend in your head when you read these words?

Read 2: Prosody

- Model reading page 10 to the children, emphasising the word **all**.
- Let children take turns to read the text on pages 20 and 21. Discuss the words they chose to emphasise and the effects.
- Bonus content: Challenge the children to read the title and labels on pages 26 and 27 with a clear voice and varied tone, as if they are giving a presentation.

Read 3: Comprehension

- Ask the children to tell you what they already knew about the ancient Romans. What facts do they remember?
- Ask the children what they have learnt about life in ancient Rome. Use the pictures on pages 30 and 31 as prompts.
- Turn to page 16 and point to the phrase **piled in**. Discuss its meaning in the context of the large number of people who could fit in the Colosseum. Ask: What other phrase could we use? (e.g. *crowded/squeezed/tumbled in*)
- Ask questions to encourage the children to compare different aspects of life in Rome. Ask:
  - ○ What did rich people have that others didn't? Discuss and compare the information on pages 6–7, 8–9 and 11.
  - ○ How is life different for a man, compared with a woman? (e.g. *most women stayed at home; men had more power than women and while men could vote, women couldn't*)
  - ○ What were events in the Colosseum like, compared with events in a stadium today?
- Bonus content: Look together at pages 26 and 27. Have the children ever seen any Roman objects, e.g. on television or at a museum? What do they think was the most important thing Romans left behind?